U.S. ENVIRONMENTAL PROTECTION AGENCY
OFFICE OF INSPECTOR GENERAL

Catalyst for Improving the Environment

Compendium of Unimplemented Recommendations
as of September 30, 2009

Report No. 10-N-0018

October 28, 2009

Abbreviations

BRAINS	Billing & Reimbursable Accounting Information Network System
CBR	Clean Water State Revolving Fund Benefits Reporting System
CIO	Chief Information Officer
CWS	Community Water Systems
EPA	U.S. Environmental Protection Agency
ESD	Explanation of Significant Differences
FACT	Financing Alternatives Comparison Tool
FCID	Food Commodity Intake Database
FY	Fiscal Year
ICR	Information Collection Request
IP	Internet Protocol
LDEQ	Louisiana Department of Environmental Quality
MATS	Management Audit Tracking System
MOU	Memorandum of Understanding
mLINQS	Relocation Expense Management System
NCC	National Computer Center
NHANES	National Health and Nutrition Examination Survey
NIST	National Institute of Standards and Technology
NSQS	National Sediment Quality Survey
OAR	Office of Air and Radiation
OARM	Office of Administration and Resources Management
OCFO	Office of the Chief Financial Officer
OECA	Office of Enforcement and Compliance Assurance
OEI	Office of Environmental Information
OIG	Office of Inspector General
OMB	Office of Management and Budget
OPP	Office of Pesticide Programs
OPPTS	Office of Prevention, Pesticides, and Toxic Substances
ORD	Office of Research and Development
OSRTI	Office of Superfund Remediation and Technology Innovation
OSWER	Office of Solid Waste and Emergency Response
OTOP	Office of Technology Operations and Planning
OU2	Operable Unit 2
OW	Office of Water
PADEP	Pennsylvania Department of Environmental Protection
POTW	Publicly Owned Treatment Works
PRB	Permeable Reactive Barrier
ROD	Record of Decision
SCORPIOS	Superfund Cost Recovery Package Imaging and On-line System
SP	Special Publication
USDA	U.S. Department of Agriculture
VMT	Vulnerability Management Tool
WCF	Working Capital Fund
YCSWRA	York City Solid Waste Refuse Agency

October 28, 2009

MEMORANDUM

SUBJECT: Compendium of Unimplemented Recommendations as of September 30, 2009
Report No. 10-N-0018

TO: Deputy Administrator
Assistant Administrators
Regional Administrators
General Counsel
Chief Financial Officer
Associate Administrators

Attached is the semiannual Compendium of Unimplemented Recommendations as of September 30, 2009, prepared by the Office of Inspector General (OIG) of the U.S. Environmental Protection Agency (EPA). This Compendium fulfills the requirement of the Inspector General Act, as amended, to identify reports containing significant recommendations described in previous Semiannual Reports to Congress on which corrective action has not been completed.

This Compendium, issued in conjunction with the Semiannual Report to Congress and as a separate document to EPA leadership, is part of the OIG's follow-up strategy to promote robust internal controls. Follow-up is done in collaboration with the EPA Office of the Chief Financial Officer and EPA Audit Follow-up Coordinators. The goal is to improve overall audit management by helping EPA managers gain a greater awareness of outstanding agreed-to commitments for action on OIG report recommendations. Implementing these recommendations will correct weaknesses, reduce vulnerabilities to risk, and leverage opportunities for improved performance.

The significance of audit follow-up, as described by the Office of Management and Budget (OMB) Circular A-50, is enhanced by the public's expectation for greater transparency and a heightened interest by Congress in realizing potential opportunities for improvement in the Federal Government. The OIG's previous Compendium reports appear to be having the intended effect of increasing Agency awareness and action on unimplemented OIG recommendations.

We selected the unimplemented recommendations listed in this Compendium based on their significance and their status in EPA's Management Audit Tracking System. In addition, some unimplemented recommendations were identified through review by the OIG. Exclusion from the Compendium does not indicate the OIG determined the corrective action to be complete for a recommendation. However, it is a goal of the OIG to verify as many significant recommendations reported as being complete as possible, through other reviews.

According to OMB Circular A-50, audit follow-up is a shared responsibility between the Agency and the OIG. We will continue to identify unimplemented recommendations for attention and action, as well as remove the listing of recommendations as unimplemented when appropriate information of completion is provided. We hope that you find this tool useful in identifying ways to further improve Agency operations.

Bill A. Roderick
Acting Inspector General

Table of Contents

Introduction

Purpose

The purpose of this Compendium of Unimplemented Recommendations is to highlight for U.S. Environmental Protection Agency (EPA) management significant recommendations that have remained unimplemented past the due date agreed upon by EPA and the Office of Inspector General (OIG). In addition, the Compendium satisfies part of Section 5(a) of the Inspector General Act of 1978, as amended, which requires each Inspector General to issue semiannual reports to Congress and include "an identification of each significant recommendation described in previous semiannual reports on which corrective action has not been completed." This Compendium is being issued in conjunction with the OIG Semiannual Report to Congress for the reporting period April 1, 2009, through September 30, 2009. The OIG intends to issue this Compendium each semiannual reporting period. The Compendium will keep Agency management informed about EPA's outstanding commitments and its progress in taking agreed-upon corrective actions on OIG recommendations to improve programs and operations.

Background

Recommendations are issued by EPA's OIG to improve the economy, efficiency, effectiveness, or integrity of EPA programs and operations. Office of Management and Budget (OMB) Circular A-50, *Audit Followup*, affirms that corrective action taken by management on resolved findings and recommendations is essential to improve the effectiveness and efficiency of government operations and that audit follow-up is a shared responsibility of agency management officials and auditors.

OMB Circular A-50 requires each agency to establish systems to ensure the prompt and proper resolution and implementation of audit recommendations. EPA Order 2750, based on OMB Circular A-50, details EPA's policy and procedures on audit follow-up. The Chief Financial Officer is the Agency Audit Follow-up Official and is responsible for Agency-wide audit resolution and ensuring Action Officials implement corrective actions. EPA uses the Management Audit Tracking System (MATS) to track information on Agency implementation of OIG recommendations. The Office of the Chief Financial Officer maintains and operates MATS. MATS receives report data, such as the report title and issue date, from the Inspector General Enterprise Management System.

The Audit Management Official in the Office of the Administrator, the Office of General Counsel, and each Assistant Administrator's or Regional Administrator's office designates an Audit Follow-up Coordinator for that office. Audit Follow-up Coordinators are responsible for quality assurance and analysis of tracking system data. When corrective actions in response to recommendations in an audit report are completed and certified, the Agency may inactivate that report's MATS file and it must no longer be tracked by the Audit Follow-up Coordinator. The Agency self-certifies that corrective actions are completed. Under the Inspector General Act, the Agency is also responsible for reporting on audit reports for which final corrective action has not been taken within 1 year or more after the Agency's management decision on corrective actions to be taken in response to findings and recommendations.

This is the third edition of the Compendium of Unimplemented Recommendations. It identifies 44 unimplemented recommendations from 26 reports compared to 32 unimplemented recommendations from 18 reports identified in the second edition for the period ending March 31, 2009. Of the 44 unimplemented recommendations currently reported, 13 from 9 reports are continuing, and 31 from 18 reports are newly identified. Also, we removed 19 unimplemented recommendations from 10 reports included in the previous Compendium. Please note that removal of an unimplemented recommendation does not imply that it was verified as implemented, but rather, it was reported as being completed or that the target completion date has been revised with OIG approval.

Scope and Methodology

Due to our limited scope and purpose, we did not conduct our work in accordance with all generally accepted government auditing standards issued by the Comptroller General of the United States. Specifically, we did not evaluate management controls, determine compliance with laws and regulations, or develop findings and recommendations. Further, we did not thoroughly assess the validity and reliability of data obtained from the Agency's MATS, which is used by EPA to track audit follow-up information. Although MATS was our primary source for identifying unimplemented recommendations, we did perform additional steps to search for unimplemented recommendations that may not have been identified in MATS.

We reviewed selected audit and evaluation reports issued by the EPA OIG from October 1, 1997, through March 31, 2009, to identify significant unimplemented recommendations for inclusion in the Compendium. We did not identify any significant unimplemented recommendations from fiscal years (FY) 1998 through 2003. We did not review recommendations from reports without an OIG agreement on the Agency's corrective action plan (Management Decision). A list of these reports can be found in Appendix 2 of the OIG Semiannual Report to Congress.

We excluded recommendations with future milestone dates for action. Some unimplemented recommendations that were excluded from this Compendium may, upon further review, be included in the next Compendium. A recommendation's exclusion from the Compendium does not indicate our determination that the recommendation has been implemented. We limited the unimplemented recommendations included in this Compendium to those we believe could have a material impact on the economy, efficiency, effectiveness, or integrity of EPA programs and operations. For this purpose, we define the following terms:

- **Economy:** Opportunity to save, prevent loss, or recover at least $500,000 in monetary costs or value.
- **Efficiency:** Improvement in the process, capacity, accessibility, or delivery of program objectives and the elimination of unnecessary or unproductive actions or expenses.
- **Effectiveness:** Improvement in the quality of, or reduction in the risk to, public health and the environment.
- **Integrity:** Improvement in operational accountability, enforcement of and compliance with laws and regulations, and security of resources for public confidence.

The following EPA offices have unimplemented recommendations listed in this Compendium:

Office of Air and Radiation (OAR)
Office of Administration and Resources Management (OARM)
Office of the Chief Financial Officer (OCFO)
Office of Enforcement and Compliance Assurance (OECA)
Office of Environmental Information (OEI)
Office of Prevention, Pesticides and Toxic Substances (OPPTS)
Office of Solid Waste and Emergency Response (OSWER)
Office of Water (OW)
Region 3
Region 4
Region 6

We anticipate that the Agency will provide updates in MATS on the status of each unimplemented recommendation, including a description of progress and an explanation of the delay in completing an agreed-to action.

Unimplemented Recommendations

Action Office: **OEI**
Report Title: **EPA Can Improve Managing of Working Capital Fund Overhead Costs**
Report No.:   **09-P-0129**   **Date Issued: 03/30/2009**

Report Summary

The Working Capital Fund (WCF) provides a centralized source of administrative and support services for EPA. The WCF strives to reduce the costs of these services in the Agency through improved efficiencies gained by achieving economies of scale, greater consumer bargaining power, and reduction in overhead. The OIG conducted this audit to determine what costs were included in the WCF overhead and the value added by the overhead costs, and to identify opportunities for WCF cost savings. While the OIG did not identify any significant cost savings for the WCF, did identify two areas requiring management attention. These areas include the documenting of the WCF staffing process and the unreasonable allocation of WCF employee time.

Unimplemented Recommendations

Recommendation 1: We recommend that the Director, OEI Office of Technology Operations and Planning (OTOP) document the OTOP WCF staffing process and methodology by developing a policy that details the process.

> *Status:* Currently, the WCF staffing process is documented in each year's budget development working files. During the FY 2010 budget development cycle, OTOP planned to ensure that the process and methodology used in determining full time equivalent percentages charged to the different WCF cost centers is clearly documented. In addition, OTOP planned to include the relevant e-mail discussions on the formulation process as part of the formal record. The agreed-to milestone date was August 15, 2009. Corrective actions are past due for completion.

Recommendation 3: We recommend that the Director, OTOP, reduce the percentage of time charged to the WCF to reflect the time spent supervising employees who charge their time to non-WCF appropriations.

> *Status:* OTOP reviewed the percentage of time charged to the WCF for the National Computer Center management and planned to adjust the fixed account numbers to reflect a mix of WCF and appropriated percentages beginning in the FY 2010 WCF budget formulation process. The agreed-to milestone date was August 15, 2009. Corrective actions are past due for completion.

Action Office:	**Region 4**
Report Title:	**Improved Management of Superfund Special Accounts Will Make More Funds Available for Clean-ups**
Report No.:	**09-P-0119** **Date Issued: 03/18/2009**

Report Summary

EPA had not used about $65 million in Superfund special accounts that were available because it lacked some management controls. Additionally, EPA was holding more than $88 million in special account funds in reserve that could be used to support priority Superfund sites, including sites where human exposure was not under control. EPA's fragmented and uncoordinated approaches to account for these funds led to missed opportunities to fund needed Superfund clean-ups. EPA lacked visibility over the amount and use of special account funds. In previous reports, the OIG had recommended that about $59 million of the $65 million of idle special account funds be reclassified or transferred to the Hazardous Substance Superfund Trust Fund (Trust Fund). In this report, OIG recommends that the remaining approximately $6.6 million be reclassified or transferred to the Trust Fund.

EPA has addressed various aspects of managing special accounts. However, improvements in EPA oversight and management of some accounts are needed to ensure Agency guidance is followed and the significant amount of money in Superfund special accounts is properly managed to support Superfund clean-up needs. EPA has not established the management controls needed to address the challenge of managing the $1.1 billion it currently has in 819 Superfund special accounts. Report recommendations were issued to OA, OSWER, OECA and Regions 1, 2, 4, 6, 7 and 10. However, Region 4 is responsible for implementing the past-due corrective action.

Unimplemented Recommendation

Recommendation 4: We recommend that the Region 4 Administrator reclassify or transfer to the Trust Fund, as appropriate, $642,283 in idle special account funds.

> *Status*: Region 4 agreed to reclassify or transfer $642,283 in idle special account funds by September 30, 2009. Corrective actions are past due for completion.

Action Office: OEI
Report Title: **Results of Technical Network Vulnerability Assessment: EPA Headquarters**
Report No.: **09-P-0097** **Date Issued: 02/23/2009**

Report Summary

The OIG contracted with Williams, Adley & Company, LLP, to conduct the annual audit of EPA's compliance with the Federal Information Security Management Act. Williams, Adley & Company, LLP, conducted the network vulnerability testing of the Agency's local area network located at EPA's Headquarters in Washington, DC. Test results identified 391 Internet Protocol (IP) addresses that contained vulnerabilities, and EPA could only identify 118 of the IP addresses. This prevented EPA from taking immediate actions to address the identified vulnerabilities. The report also forwards several medium-risk vulnerabilities identified at the EPA Region 9 office that require action by Headquarters personnel to remediate. OEI developed a corrective action plan to address the recommendations. Due to the sensitive nature of this report's technical findings, the full report is not available to the public.

Unimplemented Recommendations

Williams, Adley & Company, LLP, recommends that EPA should:

- Develop and implement procedures to update the IP registry database with information that identifies the owner of the network resource and review the database regularly for accuracy and completeness.
- Take steps to remediate all unresolved security weaknesses at EPA Headquarters and Region 9 and create a Plan of Actions and Milestones.
- Perform a technical vulnerability assessment test of Headquarters network and managed assets at Region 9.

Status: OEI stated in its response to the report that it had completed some corrective actions to address the report recommendations. Subsequently, OEI reported that problems with Region 9 software had been resolved. In response to Bullet 3, OEI plans to complete a re-scan in December 2009. Other corrective actions are also past due for completion.

Action Offices: **OARM, OEI**
Report Title: **Results of Technical Network Vulnerability Assessment: EPA's Research
Triangle Park Campus**
Report No.:   **09-P-0055**   **Date Issued: 12/09/2008**

Report Summary

The OIG contracted with Williams, Adley & Company, LLP, to conduct the annual audit of
EPA's compliance with the Federal Information Security Management Act. Williams, Adley &
Company, LLP, conducted the network vulnerability testing of the Agency's local area network
located at the EPA Research Triangle Park Campus in North Carolina. Vulnerability testing
identified IP addresses with high-risk and medium-risk vulnerabilities. Report recommendations
were issued to OARM, Office of Research and Development (ORD), and OEI. ORD certified in
MATS that it completed its corrective actions. Due to the sensitive nature of this early warning
report's technical findings, the full report is not available to the public.

Unimplemented Recommendations

Williams, Adley & Company, LLP, recommends that the Director of the National Computer
Center, OEI, and the Director of the Office of Information Resources Management Division,
OARM, at Research Triangle Park:

- Complete actions to address all unresolved vulnerability findings.
- Update EPA's Automated Security Self Evaluation and Remediation Tracking System in
  accordance with the EPA Procedure for Information Security Plans of Actions and
  Milestones for the vulnerabilities not resolved within the required timeframes.
- Perform a technical vulnerability assessment test of Research Triangle Park Campus
  network assets to demonstrate that corrective actions have resolved the vulnerabilities.

Status: OARM stated in MATS that its remaining vulnerabilities would be corrected by
May 1, 2009. According to MATS, OARM's and OEI's corrective actions have not been
completed. OEI plans to perform the technical vulnerability assessment by December 21,
2009.

Action Office:	**Region 6**
Report Title:	**EPA's Safety Determination for Delatte Metals Superfund Site Was Unsupported**
Report No.:	**09-P-0029** **Date Issued: 11/19/2008**

Report Summary

EPA's protection determination for the Delatte Metals Superfund Site was not supported by its data. Despite evidence of potential remedy failure, EPA Region 6 determined in November 2007 that conditions at Delatte protect humans and the environment in the short-term. Our review showed (a) the permeable reactive barrier (PRB) was not treating all of the shallow contaminated groundwater before it discharges to surface water and migration of metal contaminants was uncontrolled; (b) metal concentrations in surface water greatly exceeded site clean-up standards; (c) site access was uncontrolled and public warning that the Site is restricted to industrial use was limited; (d) Region 6 did not perform sufficient testing of the groundwater and surface water to determine whether contaminants were controlled; (e) Region 6 did not perform the required inspection of the PRB. EPA research scientists also raised concerns about the effectiveness of the PRB in controlling the migration of all metals and recommended that Region 6 conduct additional testing. The data available to Region 6 when it conducted its November 2007 Five-Year Review, combined with the OIG's results, show that the Site's safety cannot be determined until the effectiveness of the PRB and the risk posed by the migration of metals are assessed.

Unimplemented Recommendations

Recommendation 2-2: We recommend that the Region 6 Administrator publish EPA's milestones for obtaining the information required to make an accurate determination on the effectiveness of the Site's remedy and on the risk associated with continued metal migration.

> ***Status:*** Region 6 completed the draft optimization report in March 2009 and it is currently in review. The EPA Superfund Remediation and Technology Innovation Office and the Louisiana Department of Environmental Quality (LDEQ) expected to complete the optimization report by September 30, 2009.
>
> EPA and LDEQ plan to issue an addendum to the First Five-Year Review, acknowledging the need for additional data before a determination regarding the protectiveness related to the migration of metals can be made. The addendum will address additional steps EPA should take to assure that the remedy remains protective. EPA and LDEQ expected to publish the addendum in September 2009 along with a public notice in the local newspaper. Corrective actions are past due for completion.

Recommendation 2-4: We recommend that the Region 6 Administrator implement a comprehensive evaluation of the effectiveness of the PRB to minimize the migration of metals in groundwater off the Site and implement an appropriate response. We also recommend that the Region 6 Administrator evaluate the impact of groundwater bypassing the PRB.

> ***Status:*** Region 6 planned that the optimization report to address Recommendation 2-2 would also address Recommendation 2-4.

Action Office: OCFO
Report Title: **Audit of EPA's Fiscal 2008 and 2007 Consolidated Financial Statements**
Report No.:   **09-1-0026**   **Date Issued: 11/14/2008**

Report Summary

Our primary objectives for the financial statements audit were to determine whether EPA's consolidated financial statements were fairly stated in all material respects, EPA's internal controls over financial reporting were in place, and EPA management complied with applicable laws and regulations. The OIG rendered an unqualified, or clean, opinion meaning that the statements were fairly presented and free of material misstatement. However, the OIG reported eight significant deficiencies. The OIG also identified noncompliances with regulations relating to the Anti-Deficiency Act, the Prompt Payment Act, and reconciling intragovernmental transactions. Report recommendations were issued to OCFO, OEI, OARM, and OA. However, OCFO is the responsible office for implementing the past-due corrective action.

Unimplemented Recommendation

Recommendation 27: We recommend that OCFO through its Office of Financial Services continue to work with other federal trading partners to help reconcile the Agency's intragovernmental transactions and make appropriate adjustments to comply with federal financial reporting requirements.

> *Status***:** The Cincinnati Finance Center planned to continue its efforts and work with other federal trading partners to help reconcile the Agency's intragovernmental transactions regarding this government-wide issue. OCFO reports that EPA has made great strides and continues to reconcile the intragovernmental transactions with its trading partners. EPA has identified all material and non-material differences, which primarily relate to timing, methodology, and policy differences among its trading partners. This is a government-wide issue that continues to be an ongoing challenge. Since the differences have been identified for this year, EPA plans to discuss with the OIG the possibility of closure for this year based on identification of differences and establishing this as a new finding in future audits until this government-wide problem is resolved. The agreed-to completion date was September 30, 2009. Corrective action is past due for completion.

Action Office: OW
Report Title: EPA Assisting Tribal Water Systems but Needs to Improve Oversight
Report No.: 08-P-0266   Date Issued: 09/16/2008

Report Summary

EPA, rather than the States, has the responsibility for protecting human health and the environment on tribal lands. Approximately 600 tribal community water systems (CWS) serve an estimated 622,000 people. EPA staff members provide these systems with technical and other assistance so that tribal CWSs maintain compliance with Safe Drinking Water Act requirements. OIG conducted this evaluation to assess EPA's oversight and assistance of tribal CWSs, and to independently evaluate water quality at selected drinking water systems.

Tribal drinking water sample results in EPA files indicate that drinking water supplies consistently met regulatory requirements. Regional EPA staff also made correct compliance decisions with sample results that tribal CWSs provided. However, the OIG found internal control deficiencies existed in administering EPA's oversight of tribal CWSs in two of the five regions we reviewed. To varying degrees, tribal drinking water records in four of the five regions were incomplete due to a failure to maintain oversight of system operations and/or poor records management.

Unimplemented Recommendation

Recommendation 2-3: We recommend that the Assistant Administrator, OW, direct regions to issue monitoring and reporting violations, take appropriate enforcement actions against tribal CWSs with health-based violations or who fail to monitor or submit monitoring reports, and enter violations into Safe Drinking Water Information System.

> *Status*: OW planned to issue guidance regarding expectations of regions implementing the tribal drinking water program that they should follow the same requirements and guidance that EPA developed for States. The agreed-to completion date was September 25, 2009. Corrective action is past due for completion.

Action Office:	**OSWER**
Report Title:	**EPA Should Continue Efforts to Reduce Unliquidated Obligations in Brownfields Pilot Grants**
Report No.:	**08-P-0265** **Date Issued: 09/16/2008**

Report Summary

EPA is taking action to reduce unliquidated obligations under brownfields grants. EPA recently emphasized the need to close old grants. As a result, regions are deobligating funds on some grants. Unliquidated obligations decreased from about $29.8 million in November 2007 to about $20.9 million in March 2008, almost 30 percent.

Nonetheless, 48 grants more than 5 years old were still open as of March 2008. Of the almost $11 million of unliquidated funds reviewed in Regions 2 and 4, the regions deobligated $1.3 million (almost 12 percent) during our audit. Up to an additional $6.8 million could be available for deobligation for the 21 grants that have ended or were scheduled to end by September 30, 2008. For grants awarded prior to October 1, 2002, EPA puts deobligated Superfund funds back into the national Superfund account. EPA can then use the funds for other projects.

EPA had not consistently implemented a national policy or process that provides reasonable assurance that brownfields grant funds will be spent in a timely manner. EPA Headquarters has not provided specific guidelines on when grants should be terminated, nor has it defined inadequate progress for grant performance. Regions have generally allowed time extensions when grantees requested them.

Long periods between awarding and expending grant funds indicate that EPA is not maximizing its resources. Rather than sitting idle, awarded funds could be put to better use by communities that are ready to proceed with assessment and clean-up activities. Also, as awarded funds go unspent over time, the purchasing power of those dollars decreases.

Unimplemented Recommendation

Recommendation 3: We recommend that the Assistant Administrator, OSWER, follow up to ensure that the regions deobligate the remaining funds for the 21 grants that have ended or are scheduled to end by September 30, 2008.

> *Status:* OSWER planned to have a total of 14 cooperative agreements closed by September 30, 2009. According to MATS, as of September 30, 2009, 12 of the original 14 are closed.

Action Office:	Region 3
Report Title:	EPA Decisions to Delete Superfund Sites Should Undergo Quality Assurance Review
Report No.:	08-P-0235

Date Issued: 08/20/2008

Report Summary

As of September 2007, EPA had deleted 322 sites from the National Priorities List. Among the eight sites OIG reviewed, documentation for the Agency's decision to delete three sites was not consistent with EPA guidance. The Agency's decisions for two of these sites were also not consistent with criteria specified by EPA guidance and not supported by data and analysis. EPA did not ensure cleanup activities and goals were complete and remedies were fully protecting human health and the environment before deleting these two sites.

EPA has conducted limited national oversight of deletion decisions made by EPA's regional offices. National review of deletions is limited because regions do not always submit required information. When reviews of decisions and documents did occur, EPA did not verify that sites met criteria specified in Agency guidance. Other reasons for the deletion problems include misinterpretation or noncompliance with deletion requirements. The report was issued to OSWER, Region 3 and Region 5. However, OSWER and Region 5 have no past-due corrective actions recorded in MATS.

Unimplemented Recommendations

Recommendation 2-4: We recommend that the Region 3 Administrator conduct an analysis to determine whether the current groundwater response action at the York County Solid Waste and Refuse Agency (YCSWRA) site provides the same level of protection to human health and the environment as the response specified in EPA's Record of Decision (ROD) prior to its modification in 2004. If the current response is less protective, reinstate appropriate response requirements in EPA's ROD for the site.

> **Status:** Region 3 agreed to document the region's analysis that the current groundwater cleanup goals for restoring groundwater to beneficial use (1984 Pennsylvania Department of Environmental Protection (PADEP) agreement) is protective of human health and the environment in an Explanation of Significant Differences (ESD) that would be publicly issued by July 30, 2009.
>
> EPA has determined a ROD Amendment is necessary for the Site, and is currently conducting an internal review prior to sending it to PADEP for review/concurrence. Region 3 reported that the draft ROD Amendment essentially reinstates the groundwater criteria that were eliminated in the 2004 ESD and establishes a modified list of contaminants of concern and associated performance standards.[1] The target date for issuance of the proposed plan describing the modification is November 30, 2009, and the target date for the ROD Amendment is January 31, 2010.

---

[1] For further information on these cleanup issues, see Chapter 2 in Report No. 08-P-0235
http://www.epa.gov/oig/reports/2008/20080820-08-P-0235.pdf

Recommendation 2-5: We recommend that the Region 3 Administrator correct the inconsistency between the cleanup goals for the current groundwater response for the YCSWRA site and the cleanup requirements specified in EPA's ROD.

> *Status*: Region 3 reported that corrective actions for Recommendation 2-4 will also address Recommendation 2-5.

Recommendation 3-1: We recommend that the Region 3 Administrator work with the State of Pennsylvania to ensure that necessary response actions are taken under the appropriate regulatory authority to address groundwater contamination at Operable Unit 2 (OU2) of the McAdoo Associates site. The response actions should include appropriate controls limiting human exposure to the groundwater.

> *Status*: Region 3 agreed to conduct a comprehensive review of the site using PADEP data, to determine appropriate response actions for groundwater contamination, groundwater monitoring requirements, and inspection frequency at OU2. The evaluation was completed by April 30, 2009. According to Region 3, the response actions, monitoring requirements and inspection frequency are specified in the ESD, which recently went through a public comment period and is expected to be finalized by October 31, 2009. The agreed-to completion date was April 30, 2009.
>
> Region 3 reported it agreed to select additional institutional controls to protect the monitoring wells and prevent potable use of groundwater to OU2 by April 30, 2009. The PADEP has reviewed and concurred on the draft ESD for the Site, which calls for, among other things, establishment of institutional controls to limit human exposure to contaminated groundwater at the Site.

Action Office: **Region 3**
Report Title: **EPA Needs to Better Report Chesapeake Bay Challenges – A Summary Report**
Report No.:   **08-P-0199**   **Date Issued: 07/14/2008**

Report Summary

Despite many noteworthy accomplishments by the Chesapeake Bay partners, the Bay remains degraded. This has resulted in continuing threats to aquatic life and human health, and citizens being deprived of the Bay's full economic and recreational benefits. Through its reporting responsibilities, EPA could better advise Congress and the Chesapeake Bay community that the Bay program is significantly short of its goals and partners need to make major changes if goals are to be met. Current efforts will not enable partners to meet their goal of restoring the Bay by 2010. Further, new challenges are emerging. Bay partners need to address:

- uncontrolled land development
- limited implementation of agricultural conservation practices
- limited control over air emissions affecting Bay water quality

EPA does not have the resources, tools, or authorities to fully address all of these challenges. Farm policies, local land development decisions, and individual life styles have huge impacts on the amount of pollution being discharged to the Bay. EPA needs to further engage local governments and watershed organizations in efforts to clean up the Bay. This report summarizes several evaluations conducted by the OIG. Recommendations are addressed to the EPA Administrator. However, Region 3 is implementing the corrective actions.

Unimplemented Recommendation

Recommendation 1: We recommend that the EPA Administrator improve reporting to Congress and the public on the actual state of the Chesapeake Bay and actions necessary to improve its health by including the following information in an appropriate report:

a) activities and resources necessary to accomplish the *Chesapeake 2000* agreement goals,
b) activities that are not supported with funding or a commitment from the responsible federal, State, or local government,
c) challenges significantly hindering the Bay partners in adequately reducing nutrients and sediment,
d) milestones for generating funding and accomplishing activities, and
e) impact on the health of the Bay if milestones are not accomplished.

Status: Region 3 reports that corrective actions to address parts c, d, and e of Recommendation 1 have been completed. To address parts a and b, Region 3 planned to:

- Publish a Federal Register notice announcing an Information Collection Request (ICR) to enable collection of activities and funding information beginning in fall 2009 from additional States, local governments and non-governmental organizations. The agreed-to completion date was June 30, 2009. Region 3 reports that OMB approved an emergency ICR for 6 months on August 17, 2009, and a Federal Register notice for a 3-year renewal of the ICR is expected to be published in October.

- Include, for the first time, financial and geographic summary information in the Web-based annual health and restoration assessment report for 2009. Region 3 reports that the geographic information has been included. The financial portion is delayed and is expected to be available by October 30, 2009. The agreed-to completion date was April 15, 2009.

Action Offices: CFO, OECA
Report Title: **EPA Can Recover More Federal Superfund Money**
Report No.:   08-P-0116   **Date Issued: 03/26/2008**

Report Summary

The Comprehensive Environmental Response, Compensation, and Liability Act (Superfund) authorizes the Federal Government, States, and private parties to recover Superfund cleanup expenses (costs) from potentially responsible parties. When EPA conducts such cleanup and oversight work, it takes actions to recover those costs from responsible parties. OIG evaluated EPA's Superfund cost recovery and billing practices at a sample of National Priority List sites and found that EPA regions have recovered $165 million of $294 million (56%) of the total Superfund costs from those sites. Potentially responsible parties at these sites have generally paid what they have been billed, but EPA has not recovered as much as $129 million (44%) and has determined it will not try to recover between $30 million and $90 million of this amount. This situation indicates a potentially significant breakdown in controls over Superfund cost recovery.

Unimplemented Recommendation

Recommendation 2: We recommend the EPA Chief Financial Officer and the Assistant Administrator for OECA work collaboratively to implement mechanisms to:

- Support calculation of site cost recovery efficiency - Track the resolution of each cost as determined in the annual billing process. Resolutions could include billed, not billed for a specified reason, and pending.
- Track corrections – Identify incorrect costs until they are corrected.

Both of these mechanisms could be implemented through enhancements to the Superfund Cost Recovery Package Imaging and On-Line System (SCORPIOS).

> ***Status:*** EPA planned to explore ways to enhance information systems to develop a mechanism that supports calculating cost recovery efficiency and tracking error corrections through identification and resolution. OCFO reported that on September 28, 2009, the Office of Financial Services Limited Study Executive Steering Committee met to discuss progress on SCORPIOS enhancements, the tool to be used to capture the rationale for why costs are removed from cost recovery packages. Training on these enhancements is scheduled to occur in October 2009 and evaluation of data collected from these enhancements has been extended to December 2009. Thus data needed to develop performance measures for cost recovery efficiency is not likely to be available until spring 2010. The agreed-to completion date was December 31, 2008.

Action Office: **Region 3**
Report Title: **Despite Progress, EPA Needs to Improve Oversight of Wastewater Upgrades in the Chesapeake Bay Watershed**
Report No.:   **08-P-0049**   **Date Issued: 01/08/2008**

Report Summary

Nutrient overload has been identified as the primary cause of water quality degradation within the Chesapeake Bay. Wastewater treatment facilities are responsible for approximately 20 percent of nutrient discharges into the Bay. The OIG sought to determine how well EPA is assisting its Chesapeake Bay partners in cleaning up the Bay. This report evaluates the progress in controlling discharges from wastewater treatment facilities. We found that Chesapeake Bay wastewater treatment facilities risk not meeting the 2010 deadline for nutrient reductions if key facilities are not upgraded in time.

Unimplemented Recommendation

Recommendation 2-4: We recommend that the Region 3 Administrator instruct staff to promote awareness of and use of the Financing Alternatives Comparison Tool (FACT) and other financial analysis tools within the Chesapeake Bay community.

> *Status*: EPA planned to continue to develop and implement Webcasts on the FACT for States and grantees; streamline the FACT to make it easier to use; and expand the existing user guide. Region 3 reports that the final edits to FACT "Lite" and the user guide are currently being incorporated. Since its contractor has been fully focused on refining the Clean Water State Revolving Fund Benefits Reporting System (CBR) for the last few months to account for American Recovery and Reinvestment Act data, these projects were put on the back burner. However, a majority of the modifications for CBR has been completed, and Region 3 reports that it hopes to have both FACT Lite and the user guide released by the end of the calendar year. In addition, the Region 3 State Revolving Fund Team discussed FACT and FACT Lite with each of the States during their annual reviews. The OIG approved an extension to the original completion date of October 1, 2008, to July 31, 2009.

Action Office: OCFO
Report Title: **Audit of EPA's Fiscal 2007 and 2006 (Restated) Consolidated Financial Statements**
Report No.: 08-1-0032   **Date Issued: 11/15/2007**

Report Summary

We rendered an unqualified, or clean, opinion on EPA's Consolidated Financial Statements for fiscal 2007 and 2006 (restated), meaning that they were fairly presented and free of material misstatement. The OIG noted one material weakness with EPA's Implementation of the "Currently Not Collectible" policy for accounts receivable that caused a Material Understatement of Asset Value and led to the restatement of the fiscal 2006 financial statements. Further, the OIG noted the following six significant deficiencies:

- EPA did not properly compute an allowance for doubtful accounts.
- EPA needs to improve internal controls in recording and accounting for accounts receivable.
- Key applications do not meet federal and EPA information security requirements.
- Access and security practices over critical information technology assets need improvement.
- EPA needs to improve controls over the Integrated Financial Management System Suspense Table.
- EPA did not maintain adequate documentation for obligating accounting adjustments.

Unimplemented Recommendations

Recommendation 12: We recommend that OCFO develop a contingency plan for the Billing & Reimbursable Accounting Information Network System (BRAINS) and the Relocation Expense Management System (mLINQS). The plans should be approved by management and have documented annual reviews and testing.

> *Status*: According to MATS, EPA completed development and documented contingency plans for BRAINS and mLINQS on May 21, 2008. However, during a follow-up review, OIG found that EPA had not completed the corrective actions associated with this recommendation. OEI reported that EPA conducts a table top test annually. The OIG determined this was not sufficient and said that an operational test with equipment at the site with documented results was recommended. EPA is currently working with OARM to prepare the environment for a test to be completed during FY 2010.

Recommendation 18: We recommend that the OCFO conduct and document an annual verification and validation of implemented procedures to ensure controls are implemented as intended and are effective.

> *Status*: According to MATS, OARM incorporated the verification and validation process into their contract by November 11, 2007. However, during a follow-up review, OIG found that EPA had not completed the corrective actions associated with this recommendation. The OIG also found that EPA was not performing monthly server vulnerability scanning as stated in the OARM Server Scanning standard operating procedures.

Action Office: OAR
Report Title: **ENERGY STAR Program Can Strengthen Controls Protecting the Integrity of the Label**
Report No.: **2007-P-00028**   **Date Issued: 08/01/2007**

Report Summary

The ENERGY STAR Product Labeling Program identifies and promotes energy-efficient products. To ensure the efficiency and effectiveness of the ENERGY STAR program and the integrity of its label, EPA established several processes. These processes include product specification setting and revision, product self-certification, product verification testing, and label utilization monitoring. The OIG reviewed these processes and found improvements could be made that could better assure the integrity of the ENERGY STAR label for the consumer of home and office products.

Unimplemented Recommendation

Recommendation 3-1: We recommend that the Principal Deputy Assistant Administrator, OAR, clarify the decision criteria and document the process for revising an ENERGY STAR specification, including identifying circumstances when a specification revision would not be revised, despite a high market share of qualified products.

> *Status:* EPA stated that it has revised ENERGY STAR Specification Development Guiding Principles. Completion of the corrective action was delayed because of the need to reach agreement with the Department of Energy on a clarification the OIG requested. The initial agreed-to completion date was March 31, 2008. The OIG approved an extension of the completion date to May 31, 2009. OAR reports the discussions with the Department of Energy were completed in October 2009 and a Memorandum of Understanding (MOU) is in place. The corrective action is now reported as completed. However, because completion occurred after September 30, 2009, the semiannual - reporting period cut-off date, we are including the recommendation in this Compendium.

Action Office: OECA
Report Title: **Overcoming Obstacles to Measuring Compliance: Practices in Selected Federal Agencies**
Report No.: 2007-P-00027   **Date Issued:** 01/29/2007

Report Summary

Federal regulatory agencies with missions and obstacles similar to EPA use statistical methods to generate compliance information. They use this information to monitor their enforcement and compliance programs and demonstrate program results. These Federal programs extensively use statistical methods to identify and analyze risk, set goals, develop strategies to manage the most significant risks, and report their accomplishments. While the programs the OIG reviewed face similar obstacles as OECA, they use practical approaches to overcome these obstacles that OECA could potentially apply to its programs.

We performed this review to collect successful practices from Federal agencies similar to OECA that extensively use statistical methods, including random sampling, to measure and ensure compliance and to monitor regulatory programs.

Unimplemented Recommendation

Recommendation 2-1: We recommend that the Assistant Administrator, OECA, establish a plan of action with milestones to incorporate using statistical methods to demonstrate the results of EPA's enforcement and compliance strategies.

> *Status:* OECA agreed to develop an action plan to expand use of statistically valid compliance rates for specific noncompliance patterns focused on national priorities or other important problem areas. The agreed-to completion date for this corrective action was December 31, 2008.

Action Office: **OEI**
Report Title: **EPA Could Improve Controls Over Mainframe System Software**
Report No.:   **2007-P-00008**   **Date Issued:**   **01/29/2007**

Report Summary

The OIG engaged KPMG, LLP to conduct an audit of access to and modification of the EPA's mainframe system software housed at the Agency's National Computer Center (NCC). The NCC is located at the Research Triangle Park campus in Raleigh, North Carolina. KPMG identified several weaknesses in EPA's internal controls over its mainframe system software, including:

- Roles and responsibilities were not clearly assigned.
- Change controls were not performed in accordance with Agency policies.
- Policies, procedures, and guides could be strengthened.
- Security settings for sensitive datasets and programs were not effectively configured or implemented.

Unimplemented Recommendations

Recommendation 9: We recommend that the Director, OTOP, complete efforts to update the *OEI Information Security Manual* and the *EPA Information Security Manual.* Subsequent to finalizing the changes, ensure the manuals are (1) reviewed timely by EPA management for adequacy, accuracy, and completeness; and (2) approved by EPA management in a timely manner.

> *Status:* OEI reported in MATS that resource challenges, including human resource and acquisition resource alignments, caused the original scheduled Agency Information Security Procedural Handbook to be delayed. Dedicated EPA staff have been assigned and a contract has been awarded. The agreed-to completion date for this corrective action was September 18, 2008.
>
> As an interim stopgap while development of the handbook was being planned, the EPA Chief Information Officer (CIO) issued CIO Policy Transmittal 08-005: *Agency Network Security Policy,* on November 11, 2007. This policy provided the Agency with specific references to the National Institute of Standards and Technology (NIST) Special Publication (SP) 800-37, *Guide for the Security Certification and Accreditation of Federal Information Systems;* NIST SP 800-53 Revision 1, *Recommended Security Controls for Federal Information Systems*; NIST SP 800-100, *Information Security Handbook: A Guide for Managers*; and several other related NIST publications. OEI plans to provide the Draft Agency Network Security Policy to the Quality and Information Council for approval and voting on November 30, 2009.

Recommendation 17: We recommend that the Director, OTOP, ensure that MOUs are executed, maintained on file, and kept up to date with external users connecting to EPA information resources through nodes.

Status: Work is underway to complete the documentation for MOUs. The MOUs will be maintained on file in the NCC Records Management area. The agreed-to completion date was June 26, 2007.

Action Office: OEI
Report Title: EPA Could Improve Processes for Managing Contractor Systems and Reporting Incidents
Report No.: 2007-P-00007   **Date Issued: 01/11/2007**

Report Summary

EPA uses contractors to collect and process information on its behalf. EPA's Computer Security Incident Response Capability defines the formal process by which EPA responds to computer security-related incidents. The OIG found that EPA had not established procedures to ensure identification of all contractor systems. Further, EPA had not ensured that information security requirements were accessible for the contractors and appropriately maintained. Although EPA offices were aware of the Agency's computer security incident response policy, many offices lacked local reporting procedures, had not fully implemented automated monitoring tools, and did not have access to network attack trend information necessary to implement proactive defensive measures. The report was issued to OEI and OARM. OARM reported in MATS that its one corrective action has been completed.

Unimplemented Recommendation

Recommendation 2-1: We recommend that the Assistant Administrator for Environmental Information develop and implement guidance that EPA offices can use to identify contractor systems that contain EPA data.

> *Status*: OEI reported in MATS that resource challenges, including human resource and acquisition resource alignments, caused the original scheduled *Agency Information Security Procedural Handbook* to be delayed. Dedicated EPA staff have been assigned and a contract has been awarded. The agreed-to completion date for this corrective action was September 18, 2008. MATS states that the handbook will address identifying, certifying, and accrediting contractor systems acting on behalf of the Agency. The Draft Agency Network Security Policy review has been completed and is going to the Quality and Information Council for final review.
>
> As an interim stopgap while development of the handbook was being planned, the CIO issued CIO Policy Transmittal 08-005: *Agency Network Security Policy,* on November 11, 2007. This policy provided the Agency with specific references to the NIST SP 800-37, *Guide for the Security Certification and Accreditation of Federal Information Systems;* NIST SP 800-53 Revision 1, *Recommended Security Controls for Federal Information Systems*; NIST SP 800-100, *Information Security Handbook: A Guide for Managers*; and several other related NIST publications. The policy also cited the Federal Information Processing Standards Publication 199, *Standards for Security Categorization of Federal Information and Information Systems*, to address identifying government and contractor systems acting on behalf of the government.

Action Office:	**OSWER**
Report Title:	**Existing Contracts Enabled EPA to Quickly Respond to Hurricane Katrina: Future Improvement Opportunities Exist**
Report No.:	**2006-P-00038** **Date Issued: 09/27/2006**

Report Summary

On August 29, 2005, Hurricane Katrina devastated parts of Louisiana, Mississippi, and Alabama. EPA used existing emergency response contracts, in place at that time, to send numerous personnel to the area and purchase equipment and services to support them. Although the existing contracts allowed EPA to quickly respond to Hurricane Katrina, EPA still needed to award some noncompetitive contracts, valued at about $9 million, during its Katrina response efforts. The OIG identified improvements EPA can make in future disaster responses. The report recommendations were addressed to OARM and OSWER. OARM has no past-due corrective actions recorded in MATS.

Unimplemented Recommendation

Recommendation 4-1 (Bullet 5): Recognizing that the Assistant Administrator, OSWER, has begun a process to improve EPA's response efforts for future catastrophic events based on its Katrina experience, and that the Assistant Administrator, OARM, has initiated a similar process for safeguarding equipment, we recommend that the Assistant Administrators, OSWER and OARM, consider establishing a national custodial area in the Fixed Assets System for future large-scale national disasters so that all equipment purchases can be recorded more quickly and in a central location.

> ***Status***: OSWER reported that the Equipment Module is operational, and the regions and special teams are receiving training and adding their data into the system. OSWER expects full implementation by December 31, 2009. The agreed-to completion date was December 31, 2006.

Action Office: **OW**
Report Title: **EPA Can Better Implement Its Strategy for Managing Contaminated Sediments**
Report No.:   **2006-P-00016**   **Date Issued: 03/15/2006**

Report Summary

Contaminated sediments are the soils, sands, organic matter, and other minerals that accumulate at the bottom of a water body and contain toxic or hazardous materials that may adversely affect human health and the environment. The OIG sought to determine the effectiveness and outcomes achieved from EPA's Contaminated Sediment Management Strategy. In particular, we evaluated whether federal authorities and resources provided effective solutions, and how well EPA measured strategy effectiveness and assessed contamination. The report recommendations were issued to OSWER, OW, OECA, OA and ORD. OSWER, OECA, OA and ORD have no past-due corrective actions recorded in MATS.

Unimplemented Recommendations

Recommendation 3-1: We recommend that the Assistant Administrator, OW, develop and implement a plan for future National Sediment Quality Survey (NSQS) reports that, consistent with the Water Resources Development Act, provides a comprehensive national assessment of the extent and severity of contaminated sediments. At a minimum the design should:

a.   Use a statistical sampling approach as the basis for collecting data from EPA and other sources and assessing the national extent and severity of contaminated sediments. As a cost savings alternative, consider using statistical sampling in conjunction with existing data for the national assessment. Improve the completeness and availability of sample location information (metadata), quality assurance/quality control information, and assessment parameters for future NSQS reports.

Status: OW planned to work with ORD to determine whether a statistical design for collecting contaminated sediment data would be practical. After consultation, OW determined that the resources needed for designing and implementing a survey for sediments would exceed the resources available for the program. As an alternative, if the statistical design was determined to be impractical, OW agreed to work with ORD to develop a design that provides the best national assessment based on the available data. The agreed-to completion date was spring 2007.

b.   Ensure that the National Sediment Inventory and future NSQS reports include contaminated sediment data from all major sources, including the Great Lakes National Program Office and Superfund program. At a minimum, establish a formal coordination process for acquiring contaminated sediment data from EPA program offices and applicable agencies and organizations outside EPA. Also, consider cost-effective options for acquiring and compiling contaminated sediment data maintained in paper format.

Status: OW has developed electronic transfer protocols that will allow other EPA offices, the National Oceanic and Atmospheric Administration, and States to enter contaminated sediment data into EPA's Water Quality Exchange, which can be used for the next NSQS. OW also developed, with OSWER funds, an approach for incorporating OSWER contaminated sediment data into Water Quality Exchange. Additionally, OW plans to hold a workshop on the design of the next NSQS when resources become available. The agreed-to completion date was summer 2007.

Recommendation 3-2: We recommend that the Assistant Administrator, OW, determine a reporting frequency for the NSQS report that is both useful for decision makers and achievable for EPA, disclose to Congress that EPA cannot meet the current biennial reporting requirement specified by Section 503 of the Water Resources Development Act, and provide Congress an alternative reporting schedule for consideration.

Status:

1. OW consulted with ORD experts on sediment fate and transport to determine how much time, in general, it takes for sediment contaminant concentrations to change such that the difference can be measured. The analysis considered a representative literature compilation regarding the range of deposition and degradation rates in several watersheds. This is expected to help OW to determine a reporting frequency based on science. The analysis was completed in November 2007.

2. OW conducted a preliminary survey on the needs of other EPA programs for the NSQS data and analysis. EPA expects that this issue will be a focus of discussions in the Contaminated Sediment Data Committee and at the proposed National Workshop. These discussions will enable OW to determine a reporting frequency based on the real needs of programs for this information.

3. Based on the two actions above, OW will be able to make a recommendation for an alternative reporting schedule. The agreed-to completion date was September 30, 2008.

Action Office: **OSWER**
Report Title: **EPA Can Better Manage Superfund Resources**
Report No.: **2006-P-00013** **Date Issued: 02/28/2006**

Report Summary

The Superfund Trust Fund has decreased over the years so that in FYs 2004 and 2005 all Superfund appropriations came from general tax revenue rather than the Trust Fund. Recent studies have reported shortages in funding needs for Superfund, and have identified needed improvements in how the program is managed. The OIG performed this review in response to a congressional request to evaluate Superfund expenditures at Headquarters and the regions.

EPA has been unable to allocate and manage Superfund resources for clean-up as efficiently and effectively as possible because of the way the Agency accounts for program resources, manages by functions, supplements the program with other funds, relies on an outdated workload model, and maintains unliquidated Superfund obligations and funds in special accounts. Closely aligning offices that support the Superfund program and producing program performance and cost data have been limited because EPA disperses the responsibility for allocating and managing program resources.

Unimplemented Recommendation

Recommendation 2-3 – Accounting Definitions: We recommend to the Assistant Administrator, OSWER, that EPA should agree to define costs in a manner that supports management decision making and improve their accounting of such resources to maximize achieving program goals.

Status: OSWER reported in MATS that Recommendation 2-3 is partially implemented. Two planned corrective actions addressed this recommendation. To support management decision making, EPA modified Superfund E-Facts to reflect Superfund site cost data. The module is available for use by EPA staff. This action is considered completed. OCFO is determining if the Agency's new centralized financial management system will solve the accounting definition issue. If not, OCFO may consider system adjustments. The new centralized system is planned to be operational by October 1, 2010.

Action Office: **OPPTS**
Report Title: **Opportunities to Improve Data Quality and Children's Health through the Food Quality Protection Act**
Report No.:   **2006-P-00009**   **Date Issued: 01/10/2006**

Report Summary

We performed this review to examine the impact of the Food Quality Protection Act of 1996 on the EPA's need for scientific data and predictive tools, particularly in relation to children's health. This report is the second in a series of three reports on the Act's impact on EPA regarding children's health. The OIG specifically sought in this review to determine:

- what data requirements were required by the Food Quality Protection Act;
- whether testing guidelines, requirements, and evaluation procedures allow EPA's Office of Pesticide Programs (OPP) to determine the potential adverse effects of pesticide exposure on the developing nervous system;
- what challenges OPP overcame and what opportunities exist for OPP to acquire better pesticide exposure data to aggregate risks;
- what challenges exist and what opportunities are available for OPP to improve cumulative risk assessments; and
- what opportunities exist to better manage pesticide health risk for children.

Unimplemented Recommendation

Recommendation 4-1: We recommend that the Acting Assistant Administrator for OPPTS update the dietary exposure databases used in probabilistic models for risk assessments as soon as the food consumption data from the 2003-2004 National Health and Nutrition Examination Survey (NHANES) become available in 2006. EPA should also update the Food Commodity Intake Database (FCID) with the latest food consumption survey data, and if possible use data such as the Gerber Products Company's Feeding Infants and Toddlers Study.

> *Status:* OPP has continued to collaborate with its partners in the Center for Disease Control's National Center for Health Statistics and U.S. Department of Agriculture (USDA) to transition to the new consumption data. OPP met with USDA's Human Nutrition Survey Group in December 2007 regarding using this food consumption database to develop the requisite food commodity consumption database, FCID. In 2008, OPP began discussions on a variety of statistical issues with USDA's survey statisticians on the appropriate methods for combining NHANES survey cycles. At that time, OPP decided to adjust its pace in this area to allow it to obtain more years of data from the NHANES survey such that the resulting database includes more survey respondents and is more robust. In 2009, OPP met with personnel from USDA's Nutrient Data Laboratory and has completed the majority of the recipe work. Also in 2009, OPP began working with ORD's National Center for Environmental Assessment and OW towards incorporating the updated FCID into its exposure and risk assessment software. The agreed-to completion date was December 31, 2006. OPP anticipates completing the actions for this recommendation by summer 2010.

Action Office: OW
Report Title: More Information Is Needed on Toxaphene Degradation Products
Report No.: 2006-P-00007   **Date Issued: 12/15/2005**

Report Summary

Toxaphene in the environment changes, or degrades. The resulting degradation products are different from the original toxaphene in chemical composition and how they appear to testing instruments, so they could go unreported. The analytical methods EPA uses to identify and measure toxaphene are not designed to identify toxaphene degradation products. However, a new testing method used by others specifically tests for toxaphene degradation products. The OIG believe EPA should validate, approve, and use this method. Certain toxaphene degradation products accumulate inside people. Although studies indicate that some of these degradation products may be harmful, more research is needed to determine how much of a risk these products pose to people. The report recommendations were reported to OA, OW, OSWER and ORD. OA, OSWER, and ORD have no past-due corrective actions recorded in MATS.

Unimplemented Recommendation

Recommendation 2: We recommend that the Administrator direct the Assistant Administrators, ORD, OW, and OSWER, to arrange for specific research into the dangers of tumors (i.e., cancer) and of harm to embryos posed principally by a mixture of toxaphene congeners and metabolites found in fish.

> *Status***:** OW's Office of Superfund Remediation and Technology Innovation (OSRTI) has identified the need for an assessment of toxicity data on toxaphene degradation products and has funded ORD to conduct such a study. Based on the results, OSRTI will consider the need for additional research in the context of its other Superfund research priorities. The original agreed-to milestone date was August 31, 2009.

Action Office:	**OEI**
Report Title:	**Security Configuration and Monitoring of EPA's Remote Access Methods Need Improvement**
Report No.:	**2005-P-00011** **Date Issued:** **03/22/05**

Report Summary

EPA defines "remote access" as connection to the Agency's systems from an alternate location not directly connected to the network. Two key methods EPA uses to support remote access include: Web-Mail, which allows users to connect to their electronic mail accounts via an Internet browser, and BlackBerries, which are wireless handheld devices that allow personnel to send, receive, and read electronic mail.

OIG found that system administrators did not configure EPA's Web-Mail and BlackBerry servers to provide secure remote access to the Agency's network and did not configure or update 59 percent of the Web-Mail and BlackBerry servers to mitigate vulnerabilities. The OIG also found several of the Agency's BlackBerry devices:

- were not adequately configured, secured, or monitored,
- had no password enabled,
- had functionality that would allow users to disable passwords,
- were left unattended in workstation cubicles.

Consequently, confidentiality and integrity of EPA data, as well as the availability of the network, was at risk of unintentional or intentional exploitation.

OEI previously reported in MATS that all corrective actions in response to the recommendations in this audit report were completed. However, due to recent follow-up work by the OIG (Report No. 09-P-0240), OEI has re-opened this audit and is implementing corrective actions in concert with the OIG's Office of Mission Systems.

Unimplemented Recommendations

Recommendation 2-1: We recommend that the Director, OTOP, establish processes and assign accountability for independently verifying and validating that Web-Mail and BlackBerry servers comply with published EPA policies and standards.

> *Status*: According to our recent follow-up audit, OEI should put formal processes in place and formally assign accountability for independently verifying and validating that Web-Mail servers comply with published EPA policies and standards. OEI reports in MATS that it has established the Test and Vulnerability Assessment Lab to provide the Agency with an independent verification & validation capability. The agreed-to completion date was August 31, 2009.

Recommendation 2-2: We recommend that the Director, OTOP, develop and implement a security-monitoring program that includes testing all servers, and require all system administrators to register their servers with National Technology Services Division and participate in the security-monitoring program.

Status: According to our recent follow-up audit, OEI should implement an Agency-wide vulnerability management program that includes registering and testing all servers on a regular basis (in compliance with Federal and Agency Regulations, Policies, Procedures, and Standards), and remediating vulnerabilities in a timely manner. OEI stated in MATS that the Vulnerability Management Tool (VMT) will be added to the Agency's security-monitoring suite of tools after successful demonstration and validation. The VMT was expected to be operational by August 31, 2009.

Recommendation 2-3: We recommend that the Director, OTOP, expand the Agency's security-monitoring program to include using a variety of network vulnerability scanning tools to monitor registered servers.

Status: According to our recent follow-up audit, OEI should implement processes and utilize tools to support Agency-wide vulnerability scanning of critical network. The VMT was expected to be operational by August 31, 2009.

Recommendation 2-4: We recommend that the Director, OTOP establish and implement a process to ensure program and regional offices conduct regular security monitoring that includes vulnerability scanning.

Status: According to our recent follow-up audit, OEI should establish and implement a process to ensure program and regional offices conduct regular security monitoring that includes vulnerability scanning. The VMT was expected to be operational by August 31, 2009.

Action Office: **OAR**
Report Title: **Substantial Changes Needed in Implementation and Oversight of Title V Permits If Program Goals Are to Be Fully Realized**
Report No.:   **2005-P-00010**   **Date Issued: 03/09/2005**

Report Summary

Title V of the Clean Air Act, designed to reduce violations and improve enforcing air pollution laws for the largest sources of air pollution, requires that all major stationary sources of air pollutants obtain a permit to operate. More than 17,000 sources are subject to Title V permit requirements. Our analysis identified concerns with five key aspects of Title V permits: (1) permit clarity, (2) statements of basis, (3) monitoring provisions, (4) annual compliance certifications, and (5) practical enforceability. One finding in particular relates to compliance certifications and wording on credible evidence. When EPA amended the rule on continuous or intermittent compliance,[2] a key clause on credible evidence was inadvertently left out (Recommendation 2-2 addresses this issue).

Collectively, these problems can hamper the ability of EPA, State and local regulators, and the public to understand what requirements sources are subject to, how they will be measured, and ultimately to hold sources accountable for meeting applicable air quality requirements. EPA's oversight and guidance of Title V activities have resulted in some improvements in Title V programs; however, areas needing further improvement remain.

Unimplemented Recommendations

Recommendation 2-1: We recommend that the Assistant Administrator, OAR, develop and issue guidance or rulemaking on annual compliance certification content which requires responsible officials to certify compliance with all applicable terms and conditions of the permit, as appropriate.

> *Status*: EPA stated in MATS that based on recommendations from the Clean Air Act Advisory Group Task Force on Title V Implementation, the Office of Air Quality Planning and Standards has begun developing a guidance document that will include guidance on compliance certifications. However, since FY 2005, EPA has not submitted a formal action plan to the OIG for approval stating how it plans to address this recommendation.

Recommendation 2-2: We recommend that the Assistant Administrator, OAR, issue the draft rule regarding intermittent versus continuous monitoring as it relates to annual compliance certifications and including credible evidence.

> *Status*: EPA did not concur with this recommendation, and it remains unresolved. The Agency met with the OIG in July 2009 and is providing additional information. The OIG believes this recommendation is key to knowing the basis of the permittee's reported compliance with the terms and conditions of its Title V permit that underlies its annual compliance certification.

---

[2] 40 Code of Federal Regulations 70.6 (c)(5)(iii)(B)

Recommendation 2-3: We recommend that the Assistant Administrator, OAR, develop nationwide guidance or rulemaking, as appropriate, on the contents of statements of basis which includes discussions of monitoring, operational requirements, regulatory applicability determinations, explanations of any conditions from previously issued permits that are not being transferred to the Title V permit, discussions of streamlining requirements, and other factual information, where advisable, including a listing of prior Title V permits issued to the same applicant at the plant, attainment status, and construction, permitting, and compliance history of the plant.

Status: OAR plans to work with the regions to disseminate information about the positions EPA has taken on statements of basis in response to citizens programs and permit petitions. OAR also intends to develop a plan for identifying and sharing with permitting agencies those statements of basis that represent "best practices." This effort is planned to be included in guidance documentation addressing Recommendation 2-1. However, EPA has not submitted a formal action plan to the OIG for approval stating how it plans to address this recommendation.

Recommendation 3-1: We recommend that the Assistant Administrator, OAR, promulgate the draft order of sanctions rule which provides notice to State and local agencies, as well as the public, regarding the actions that will be taken when Notices of Deficiency are not timely resolved by State and local Title V permitting authorities.

Status: EPA did not concur with this recommendation, and it remains unresolved. The Agency met with the OIG in July 2009 and is providing additional information. The OIG believes this issue involves basic program criteria needed for EPA to oversee the Title V program.

Action Office: **OW**
Report Title: **EPA Needs to Reinforce Its National Pretreatment Program**
Report No: **2004-P-00030** **Date Issued:** **09/28/2004**

Report Summary

The reductions in industrial waste discharges to the nation's sewer systems that characterized the early years of the pretreatment program have not endured. Since the middle of the 1990s, there has been little change in the volume of a broad list of toxic pollutants transferred to Publicly Owned Treatment Works (POTWs) or in the index of risk associated with these pollutants. As a result, the performance of EPA's pretreatment program, which is responsible for controlling these discharges, is threatened, and progress toward achieving the Clean Water Act goal of eliminating toxic discharges that can harm water quality has stalled. The curtailing of the early gains may be explained in part by two factors: (1) dischargers that developed systems in response to EPA's initial program requirements have not enhanced their pretreatment systems in recent years, and (2) the rate at which EPA has been issuing effluent guidelines dramatically declined since 1990. Without more visible leadership from Headquarters, improved programmatic information, and the adoption of results-based performance measures, EPA's pretreatment program is at risk of losing the gains it made in its early years.

Unimplemented Recommendation

Recommendation 4-1: We recommend that the Acting Assistant Administrator, OW, direct staff to develop a long-term strategy to identify the data it needs for developing pretreatment results-based measurements; determine the resources necessary to carry out the strategy; and gain the support of other Agency, State, and POTW staff to carry out the strategy.

> *Status*: OW agreed to request information on databases used by the EPA Regions and States to store information regarding POTW pretreatment program performance. Through the Permitting for Results process, OW will compile information regarding current data systems used to store pretreatment data at the EPA regional and State level. OW intends to use this information to identify inaccurate data and target data correction in the Permit Compliance System. Both of these activities are crucial to facilitate migration and retention of data as EPA transitions to the Integrated Compliance Information System. Once these efforts are complete, OW will be able to determine a long-term strategy based on data availability and resources, which should ultimately assist it in developing pretreatment results-based measurements. The agreed-to completion date for this corrective action was September 30, 2007.

Action Office: OEI
Report Title: EPA's Administration of Network Firewalls Needs Improvement
Report No.: 2004-P-00013   **Date Issued:** 03/31/2004

Report Summary

While OEI has taken positive actions to properly implement EPA's computer system firewalls, additional areas need to be addressed to provide greater assurance that the Agency's information resources are adequately secured. EPA uses "firewall" technology, in combination with other network security devices, as the foundation to secure information resources. EPA's "physical" security practices for the firewalls, which include continuity of operations practices and procedures, were adequate. However, logical and configuration improvements are needed. Without these improvements, hackers could circumvent EPA's network security, allowing them the potential to negatively affect integrity, confidentiality, and availability of EPA systems and data on the network.

OEI previously reported in MATS that all corrective actions in response to the recommendations in this audit report were completed. However, recent follow-up work by the OIG (Report No. 09-P-0240) identified actions OEI still needs to take to fully satisfy two of the report's recommendations.

Unimplemented Recommendations

Recommendation 2-1: We recommend that the Director, OTOP, develop and implement a standard configuration requirement for adequately securing workstations used to remotely administer network firewalls.

> *Status:* The OIG determined that OEI should complete the implementation of "proxy" servers for remote access to firewall consoles and obtain management approval for and issue the procedure developed for granting access to firewall consoles. The revised completion date was March 31, 2009.

Recommendation 3-2: We recommend that the Director, OTOP, modify the network vulnerability assessment methodology to include scanning of all firewall components (e.g., workstations, management consoles, and enforcement point servers).

> *Status:* The OIG determined that OEI should implement regular vulnerability scanning of security infrastructure. The revised completion date was September 30, 2009. The corrective action has not been completed.

Appendix A

OIG Reports with Unimplemented Recommendations by Program Office
as of September 30, 2009

OAR

2007-P-00028, ENERGY STAR Program Can Strengthen Controls Protecting the Integrity of the Label

2005-P-00010, Substantial Changes Needed in Implementation and Oversight of Title V Permits If Program Goals Are to Be Fully Realized

OARM

09-P-0055, Results of Technical Network Vulnerability Assessment: EPA's Research Triangle Park Campus

OCFO

09-1-0026, Audit of EPA's Fiscal 2008 and 2007 Consolidated Financial Statements

08-P-0116, EPA Can Recover More Federal Superfund Money

08-1-0032, Audit of EPA's Fiscal 2007 and 2006 (Restated) Consolidated Financial Statements

OECA

08-P-0116, EPA Can Recover More Federal Superfund Money

2007-P-00027, Overcoming Obstacles to Measuring Compliance: Practices in Selected Federal Agencies

OEI

09-P-0129, EPA Can Improve Managing of Working Capital Fund Overhead Costs

09-P-0097, Results of Technical Network Vulnerability Assessment: EPA Headquarters

09-P-0055, Results of Technical Network Vulnerability Assessment: EPA's Research Triangle Park Campus

2007-P-00008, EPA Could Improve Controls Over Mainframe System Software

2007-P-00007, EPA Could Improve Processes for Managing Contractor Systems and Reporting Incidents

2005-P-00011, Security Configuration and Monitoring of EPA's Remote Access Methods Need Improvement

2004-P-00013, EPA's Administration of Network Firewalls Needs Improvement

OPPTS

2006-P-00009, Opportunities to Improve Data Quality and Children's Health through the Food Quality Protection Act

OSWER

08-P-0265, EPA Should Continue Efforts to Reduce Unliquidated Obligations in Brownfields Pilot Grants

2006-P-00038, Existing Contracts Enabled EPA to Quickly Respond to Hurricane Katrina: Future Improvement Opportunities Exist

2006-P-00013, EPA Can Better Manage Superfund Resources

OW

08-P-0266, EPA Assisting Tribal Water Systems but Needs to Improve Oversight

2006-P-00016, EPA Can Better Implement Its Strategy for Managing Contaminated Sediments

2006-P-00007, More Information Is Needed on Toxaphene Degradation Products

2004-P-00030, EPA Needs to Reinforce Its National Pretreatment Program

Region 3

08-P-0235, EPA Decisions to Delete Superfund Sites Should Undergo Quality Assurance Review

08-P-0199, EPA Needs to Better Report Chesapeake Bay Challenges – A Summary Report

08-P-0049, Despite Progress, EPA Needs to Improve Oversight of Wastewater Upgrades in the Chesapeake Bay Watershed

Region 4

09-P-0119, Improved Management of Superfund Special Accounts Will Make More Funds Available for Clean-ups

Region 6

09-P-0029, EPA's Safety Determination for Delatte Metals Superfund Site Was Unsupported

Appendix B

Unimplemented Recommendations
04/30/09 Compendium Compared to Current Compendium

Continuing Unimplemented Recommendations

08-P-0116, EPA Can Recover More Federal Superfund Money **(Recommendation 2)**

2007-P-00008, EPA Could Improve Controls Over Mainframe System Software **(Recommendation 9)**

2007-P-00007, EPA Could Improve Processes for Managing Contractor Systems and Reporting Incidents **(Recommendation 2-1)**

2006-P-00038, Existing Contracts Enabled EPA to Quickly Respond to Hurricane Katrina: Future Improvement Opportunities Exist **(Recommendation 4-1(bullet 5))**

2006-P-00016, EPA Can Better Implement Its Strategy for Managing Contaminated Sediments **(Recommendations 3-1, 3-2)**

2006-P-00013, EPA Can Better Manage Superfund Resources **(Recommendation 2-3)**

2006-P-00009, Opportunities to Improve Data Quality and Children's Health through the Food Quality Protection Act **(Recommendation 4-1)**

2005-P-00010, Substantial Changes Needed in Implementation and Oversight of Title V Permits If Program Goals Are to Be Fully Realized **(Recommendations 2-1, 2-2, 2-3, 3-1)**

2004-P-00030, EPA Needs to Reinforce Its National Pretreatment Program **(Recommendation 4-1)**

New Unimplemented Recommendations

09-P-0129, EPA Can Improve Managing of Working Capital Fund Overhead Costs **(Recommendations 1, 3)**

09-P-0119, Improved Management of Superfund Special Accounts Will Make More Funds Available for Clean-ups **(Recommendation 4)**

09-P-0097, Results of Technical Network Vulnerability Assessment: EPA Headquarters **(Recommendations 1, 2, 3)**

09-P-0055, Results of Technical Network Vulnerability Assessment: EPA's Research Triangle Park Campus **(Recommendations 1, 2, 3)**

09-P-0029, EPA's Safety Determination for Delatte Metals Superfund Site Was Unsupported **(Recommendations 2-2, 2-4)**

09-1-0026, Audit of EPA's Fiscal 2008 and 2007 Consolidated Financial Statements **(Recommendation 27)**

08-P-0266, EPA Assisting Tribal Water Systems but Needs to Improve Oversight **(Recommendation 2-3)**

08-P-0265, EPA Should Continue Efforts to Reduce Unliquidated Obligations in Brownfields Pilot Grants **(Recommendation 3)**

08-P-0235, EPA Decisions to Delete Superfund Sites Should Undergo Quality Assurance Review **(Recommendations 2-4, 2-5, 3-1)**

08-P-0199, EPA Needs to Better Report Chesapeake Bay Challenges – A Summary Report **(Recommendation 1)**

08-P-0049, Despite Progress, EPA Needs to Improve Oversight of Wastewater Upgrades in the Chesapeake Bay Watershed **(Recommendation 2-4)**

08-1-0032, Audit of EPA's Fiscal 2007 and 2006 (Restated) Consolidated Financial Statements **(Recommendations 12, 18)**

2007-P-00028, ENERGY STAR Program Can Strengthen Controls Protecting the Integrity of the Label **(Recommendation 3-1)**

2007-P-00027, Overcoming Obstacles to Measuring Compliance: Practices in Selected Federal Agencies **(Recommendation 2-1)**

2007-P-00008, EPA Could Improve Controls Over Mainframe System Software **(Recommendation 17)**

2006-P-00007, More Information Is Needed on Toxaphene Degradation Products **(Recommendation 2)**

2005-P-00011, Security Configuration and Monitoring of EPA's Remote Access Methods Need Improvement **(Recommendations 2-1, 2-2, 2-3, 2-4)**

2004-P-00013, EPA's Administration of Network Firewalls Needs Improvement **(Recommendations 2-1, 3-2)**

*Removed Unimplemented Recommendations**

08-P-0141, EPA Needs to Track Compliance with Superfund Cleanup Requirements **(Recommendations 1, 5)**

08-P-0116, EPA Can Recover More Federal Superfund Money **(Recommendation 3)**

08-P-0093, EPA Should Further Limit Use of Cost-Plus-Award-Fee Contracts **(Recommendations 2-1, 2-2)**

2007-P-00030, Improved Management Practices Needed to Increase Use of Exchange Network **(Recommendations 2-2, 4-2, 5-1, 5-2)**

2007-P-00026, EPA Needs to Take More Action in Implementing Alternative Approaches to Superfund Cleanups **(Recommendation 3-1)**

2007-P-00025, EPA Can Improve Its Oversight of Audit Follow-up **(Recommendation 1)**

2006-P-00038, Existing Contracts Enabled EPA to Quickly Respond to Hurricane Katrina: Future Improvement Opportunities Exist **(Recommendations 2-1, 3-2, 4-1(bullet 2))**

2006-P-00001, Rulemaking on Solvent-Contaminated Industrial Wipes **(Recommendation 4-1)**

2005-P-00024, Limited Knowledge of the Universe of Regulated Entities Impedes EPA's Ability to Demonstrate Changes in Regulatory Compliance **(Recommendation 2-4)**

2001-P-00013, State Enforcement of Clean Water Act Dischargers Can Be More Effective **(Recommendations 3-2, 3-4, 3-5)**

* Please note that removal of an unimplemented recommendation does not imply that it was verified as implemented, but rather, it was reported as being completed or that the target completion date has been revised with OIG approval.